Sports &
Games

The Nature Company Discoveries Library published by Time-Life Books

Conceived and produced by
Weldon Owen Pty Limited
43 Victoria Street, McMahons Point,
NSW, 2060, Australia
A member of the
Weldon Owen Group of Companies
Sydney • San Francisco
Copyright 1997 © US Weldon Owen Inc.
Copyright 1997 © Weldon Owen Pty Limited

THE NATURE COMPANY
Priscilla Wrubel, Ed Strobin, Steve Manning,
Georganne Papac, Tracy Fortini

TIME LIFE BOOKS
Time-Life Books is a division of Time Life Inc.
Time-Life is a trademark of Time Warner Inc.
U.S.A.

Time-Life Custom Publishing
Vice President and Publisher: Terry Newell
Director of New Product Development:
Regina Hall
Managing Editor: Donia Ann Steele
Director of Sales: Neil Levin
Director of Financial Operations: J. Brian Birky

WELDON OWEN Pty Limited
Chairman: Kevin Weldon
President: John Owen
Publisher: Sheena Coupe
Managing Editor: Rosemary McDonald
Project Editor: Helen Bateman
Text Editor: Claire Craig
Art Director: Sue Burk
Designer: Catherine Au-Yeung
Photo Research: Annette Crueger
Illustrations Research: Amanda Weir
Production Consultant: Mick Bagnato
Production Manager: Simone Perryman

Vice President, International Sales:
Stuart Laurence
Coeditions Director: Derek Barton

Text: Neil Jameson

Illustrators: Christer Eriksson; Chris Forsey;
Ray Grinaway; Adam Hook/Bernard Thornton
Artists, UK; Christa Hook/Bernard Thornton
Artists, UK; Janet Jones; Iain McKellar;
Steve Noon/Garden Studio; Matthew Ottley;
John Richards; Roger Stewart/Brihton Illustration;
Rodger Towers/Brihton Illustration

Library of Congress
Cataloging-in-Publication Data
Jameson, Neil, 1953-
Sports / Neil Jameson.
    p. cm -- (Discoveries Library)
  Includes index.
  ISBN 0-7835-4800-1
  1. Sports--Juvenile literature. [1. Sports.]
  I. Title. II. Series.
  GV707.J36 1997
  796'.04--dc20   95-53698

Manufactured by Mandarin Offset
Printed in China

A Weldon Owen Production

THE NATURE COMPANY
DISCOVERIES
LIBRARY

Sports &
Games

CONSULTING EDITORS

Dr. Maxwell L. Howell
Emeritus Professor
University of Queensland, Australia

Dr. Murray Phillips
Lecturer, Centre for Sports Studies
University of Canberra, Australia

TIME
LIFE
BOOKS

Contents

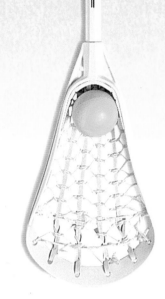

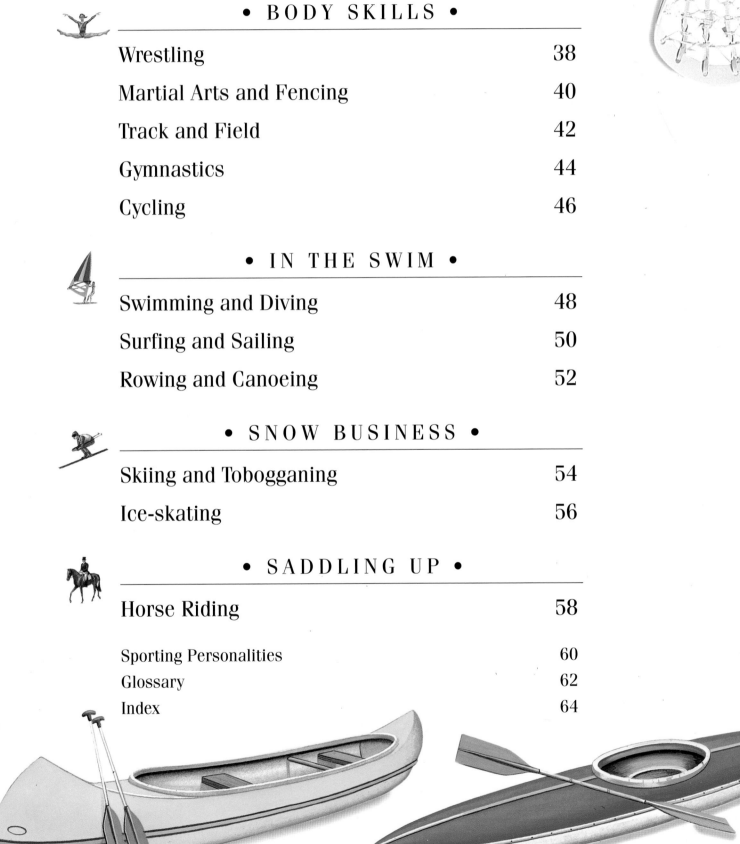

RACE IN ARMOR
The oddest foot race at the ancient Olympics—the hoplite race—was introduced in 520 BC. Contestants, naked except for their leg-protectors and helmets, had to carry their shields while they ran the race.

• INTRODUCTION •

The Beginnings of Sports

People have always enjoyed competing against each other. In prehistoric times, a hunter who could run fast and throw a stone or spear accurately was a valued member of the tribe. The ancient Greeks included athletics in many of their religious festivals. In 776 BC, they held a festival of sport to honor Zeus, the greatest of the Greek gods. Athletes from all over the country gathered in a stadium in the valley of Olympia to test their speed, strength and skill in the first Olympic Games. These games were held every four years, and for a long time only males were allowed to watch and take part in the races. The games continued for several centuries after the Romans conquered Greece, until the Roman Emperor Theodosius I ended them in AD 394. Almost 1,500 years later, the ruins of the Olympic stadium were discovered by archaeologists. Frenchman Baron Pierre de Coubertin suggested holding a modern, international Olympic Games. The first games of the new era of the Olympics were held in Athens in 1896.

HAIL THE CHAMPION
Today's victorious Olympic champions receive gold medals. Sporting heroes of ancient Greece were crowned with wreaths made from laurel leaves, as shown on this vase.

SPORTING SPECTACULAR

In 680 BC, four-horse chariot races were added to the program of the 25th Olympic Games. As many as 40 chariots crashed, jostled and maneuvered their way around the course marked out in the hippodrome.

THE OLYMPIC TORCH

The lighting of the flame is the high point of the opening ceremony at the modern Olympic Games. Since 1936, this custom has served as a reminder of the beginnings of this festival. A lighted torch is carried by relay runners from Olympia in Greece, site of the original Olympics, to the city where the modern games are to be held. This torch is used to light the Olympic flame that burns above the stadium throughout the festival. The flame is seen as a symbol of nations and athletes competing peacefully in the spirit of sport.

DISCUS HERO

Among the sports to have survived from the earliest Olympics is discus throwing. This ancient Greek vase shows a discus thrower placing or withdrawing the peg that is used to mark the distance the discus has been thrown.

• NETS AND RACKETS •

Tennis and Table Tennis

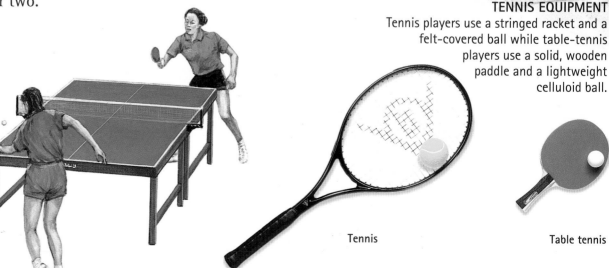

The knights who returned to France from the Crusades in the Middle East 800 years ago brought with them a ball game we now know as tennis. Europeans played this game indoors, often inside a monastery or palace. It was known as royal, real or court tennis. At first, the ball was struck with the bare hand. Later, gloves and then a bat or paddle were used. The introduction of a mesh of strings in the sixteenth century enabled royal tennis players to hit the ball with more power. A game called sphairistike, or lawn tennis, was introduced into England by Major Walter Wingfield in 1874. But the real birth of modern tennis was at Wimbledon, England, in 1877 when the All England championship, or Wimbledon tournament, was held for the first time. Today, tournaments usually take place on clay or synthetic playing surfaces, although a few are still held on grass. Tennis can be played as singles—with one player at either end of the court, or as doubles—with two players teaming up to play another two.

TENNIS EQUIPMENT
Tennis players use a stringed racket and a felt-covered ball while table-tennis players use a solid, wooden paddle and a lightweight celluloid ball.

SPEED AND SKILL
With a net and miniature court area, table tennis offers the excitement of tennis on a smaller scale.

Tennis

Table tennis

DID YOU KNOW?

Until the 1960s, most tennis players were amateurs and could not earn money from the game. Today, top players can win millions of dollars in prize money by playing on the world professional circuit.

PLAYING PING PONG

Table tennis, or ping pong, was developed in the late nineteenth century as a miniature indoor version of tennis. The trademark Ping-Pong was introduced by a supplier of early table-tennis equipment to describe the noise the ball made: "ping" when it hit the bat and "pong" when it bounced off the table. The first balls were made of rubber or cork covered with cloth. The introduction of the celluloid ball helped to make table tennis an exciting test of reflexes and skill. Today, it is played all around the world. It is especially popular in China where children learn the game on concrete tables built in schoolyards.

TENNIS COURT

A tennis court is 77.96 ft (23.77 m) long and 35.98 ft (10.97 m) wide. The net is 2.98 ft (0.91 m) high at the center.

Doubles side line
Singles side line
Service court
Center service line
Service court
Net
Base line

A GAME FOR KINGS

Royal tennis was popular from the twelfth century on. In the sixteenth century, King Henry VIII of England enjoyed the game so much that he built a court at his Hampton Court Palace.

9

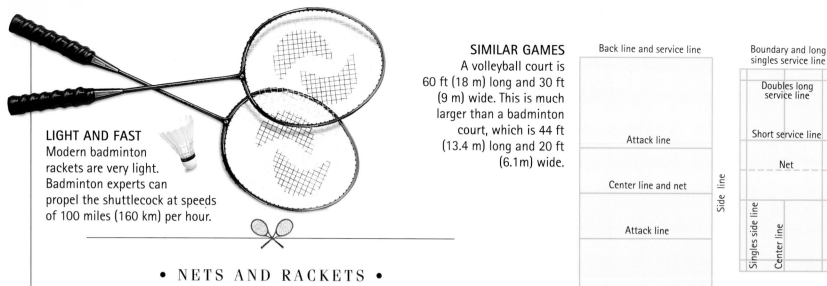

LIGHT AND FAST
Modern badminton rackets are very light. Badminton experts can propel the shuttlecock at speeds of 100 miles (160 km) per hour.

Badminton and Volleyball

In the game of badminton the players use stringed rackets to hit a shuttlecock high over a net. A player scores a point by grounding the shuttlecock on their opponent's side of the net. Games similar to badminton were played in ancient China and India. The sport was not given its name, however, until the 1870s when the Duke of Beaufort, a famous English sportsman, invited guests to play the game at his country estate–Badminton. The game of volleyball also has a high net, but its players do not use rackets. Instead, they can use any part of the body above the waist to play the ball. Most shots, however, are played with one or both hands, and players must not hold or throw the ball. There are two forms of the game. Beach volleyball is played outdoors with two players on each side. The standard version of volleyball is held on indoor courts with six players on each side.

SIMILAR GAMES
A volleyball court is 60 ft (18 m) long and 30 ft (9 m) wide. This is much larger than a badminton court, which is 44 ft (13.4 m) long and 20 ft (6.1m) wide.

Volleyball court

Back line and service line

Attack line

Center line and net

Attack line

Side line

Badminton court

Boundary and long singles service line

Doubles long service line

Short service line

Net

Singles side line

Center line

Doubles side line

TEAM PLAY
The beach volleyball player on the left has hit the ball in a shot known as a "spike." One defensive player on the opposing side is leaping to block the shot, while the other positions herself to retrieve the ball if the block fails.

SLAMMING THE SHUTTLE
Badminton is a fast game. Players have to be very agile and have quick reflexes. It can be played by two players (singles) or as a doubles contest with four players, as shown here.

WORLD STAGE
Volleyball is very popular around the world. National teams compete every four years in the Olympic Games and every two years for the World Cup. Japan, China, Cuba and the United States are all leading volleyball nations.

THE SHUTTLECOCK

Instead of a bat or a racket, ancient Chinese of the Han Dynasty played a version of badminton using their feet. The earliest shuttlecock was made from a piece of cork in which feathers were embedded. It was so unsteady in the air that it was nicknamed "the wobbler." Designers tried to come up with a shuttle that would perform in a predictable manner. They invented the barrel-shaped shuttle in 1900 and then the straight-feather shuttle nine years later. The modern "birdie" (as it is called in the United States) is made of 16 goose feathers set in a domed cork. It has a small lead weight in the base to make it move freely through the air. Mass-produced shuttles are often made of plastic.

PRISON GAME
The walls of Fleet Prison in London provided a ready-made court for eighteenth-century convicts who passed the time by playing the game of racquets.

• NETS AND RACKETS •

Squash

The sport of squash can be traced back to the 1700s to a game called racquets. It was first played by prisoners serving a sentence in London's Fleet Prison for not paying their debts. Later, the English upper classes began to play the sport. When students at Harrow, an English Public School, played the game with a soft rubber ball that could be squashed, the game became even more popular. Later, indoor courts with four walls were built. In squash, the ball can come in contact with any of the four walls, providing it hits the front wall with every shot played. The ball can also bounce off the floor, but not the roof. The game is played socially and as a competitive sport, with world championships held each year. A game very similar to squash, called racquetball, was invented in 1950 by American Joe Sobek in Greenwich, Connecticut. Like squash, racquetball is played on a four-walled court, but it is considered easier to play because its larger ball bounces higher than the smaller squash ball.

WATCH AND PLAY
Major championship matches are played on courts with walls made of thick, transparent plastic. Spectators and television cameras have a clear view of the game, but the players have a clouded view of the outside so that they are not distracted by people moving around.

THE COURT

A squash court is a fully enclosed area, 21 ft (6.40 m) wide and 32 ft (9.75 m) long. The floor and all four walls are marked with lines 2 in (5 cm) wide that indicate the playing area.

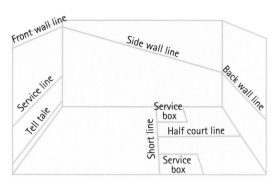

Front wall line
Side wall line
Back wall line
Service line
Tell tale
Short line
Service box
Half court line
Service box

A SPEEDING BALL

Pelota, or jai alai, is perhaps the world's fastest ball game. It is similar to squash but played on a much larger court. Instead of a racket, the players use a 3 ft (90 cm) curved basket that is attached to a glove strapped tightly at the wrist. This enables them to catch and fling the ball at extremely high speeds. Contestants sometimes wear helmets in case they are struck by the ball. The game is popular in Mexico and other Spanish-speaking countries. Although pelota means "little ball," the modern version is played with a ball the size of a baseball.

EQUIPMENT

A small ball and a lightweight racket with a long handle are used in squash. Racquetball players use a heavier racket with a shorter handle, and a larger ball.

Squash

Racquetball

HIGH ENERGY

Squash is a high-energy sport, and players need to be fit and agile. It is usually played by two people who score points by keeping the ball in play while hitting it against a wall. Players can use backhand and forehand strokes similar to tennis.

Discover more in Tennis and Table Tennis

FIELD HOCKEY
In field hockey, players must strike the ball with the flat side of the stick only. Skill and teamwork are two of the most important aspects of modern hockey.

ICE HOCKEY
Ice hockey is an Olympic sport and a major winter activity in North America and northern Europe. Goal-tenders in ice hockey wear protective clothing, including face masks, to protect themselves from injury caused by the speed of the puck.

• GOING FOR GOAL •

Hockey and Lacrosse

The game of hockey developed from the many basic games that used a stick and a ball. The ancient Greeks, Egyptians, Native Americans and Aztecs all played a similar game, as did the Irish who called it hurling. These early games were very rough, and often resembled a brawl more than a sport. The rules to the modern game of field hockey were officially introduced in England during the 1880s. It is played by two teams of men or women with 11 players on each side. Like soccer, the object of the game is to score by hitting the ball into the opposing team's goal. Ice hockey is a combination of field hockey and ice-skating and has just six players on each side. It is a very physical game and offenses, such as tripping and roughing, are penalized. The sport was devised in Canada. At first, a rubber ball was used. This was later replaced by a hard, flat rubber disk known as a puck, which can skim across the ice at great speed.

Field-hockey stick

Standard ice-hockey stick

Goal-tender's ice-hockey stick

Lacrosse stick

Side line

Goal line

Goal

Penalty spot

Shooting circle

Center line

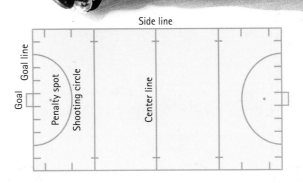

Goal line

Goal

Face-off circle

Blue line

Red line

PLAYING AREAS
The field-hockey field (left) is 300 ft (91.4 m) long and 180 ft (54.8 m) wide. The ice-hockey rink (above) can be 184–200 ft (56–61 m) long and 85–98 ft (26–30 m) wide.

BANDY-BALL
An early form of hockey known as bandy-ball is shown in a stained glass window in England's Gloucester Cathedral, built in 1360.

LACROSSE

Lacrosse is the name French settlers gave to the Native American game of baggataway. Instead of a hooked stick being used to hit the ball on the ground, a stick with a net at the end was used to fling, catch and carry the ball. In baggataway, up to 500 players took part in what often became more a battle than a game, and some were seriously injured or killed. In 1763, Pontiac, the chief of the Ottawa tribe, staged a match outside the gates of Fort Michillimackinac. When the English soldiers came out to watch, the Native Americans attacked and captured the fort. The modern rules of lacrosse were drafted in 1876 by Dr. George W. Beers, a Montreal dentist. This 1855 engraving shows Native Americans playing baggataway on ice.

SPEED GAME
Modern lacrosse is one of the fastest team sports of all. Players use a solid rubber ball that cannot be touched by the hand. In women's lacrosse, each team has 12 players, whereas men's teams have only ten.

Discover more in Soccer

HEIGHT IS MIGHT
Being tall is a great advantage for a basketball player. It is not unusual to find players in the National Basketball Association who are more than 7 ft (2.1 m) tall.

Basketball and Netball

Canadian Dr. James Naismith wanted to find a sport that his students could play indoors during icy winters in Massachusetts. In 1891, he invented basketball. This fast-action game with five players on each side is now one of the world's most popular team sports. It is particularly well supported in the United States where the best basketball players play professionally in the National Basketball Association. The aim of basketball, and netball (a similar game), is to score goals by shooting the ball through a hoop or basket positioned about 10 ft (3 m) above the ground. Basketball players can advance the ball up the court by running and bouncing it (dribbling), or by passing it to a team-mate. Netballers can only move the ball by passing it. The top netballing nations compete for the World Championship. Basketballing nations take part in the World Championship as well as the Olympic Games.

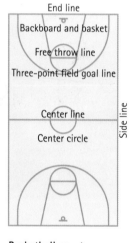

End line
Backboard and basket
Free throw line
Three-point field goal line
Center line
Center circle
Side line

Basketball court

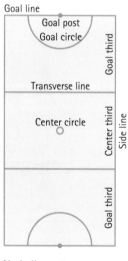

Goal line
Goal post
Goal circle
Goal third
Transverse line
Center third
Center circle
Side line
Goal third

Netball court

COURT SIZE
A netball court is 100 ft (30.5 m) long and 49.8 ft (15.2 m) wide. A basketball court is 91.8 ft (28 m) long and 49.2 ft (15 m) wide.

PASSING ON
Netball, which is played mainly by women, demands great fitness and athleticism. Australia, New Zealand and Jamaica are among the leading nations in world netball.

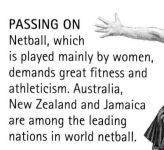

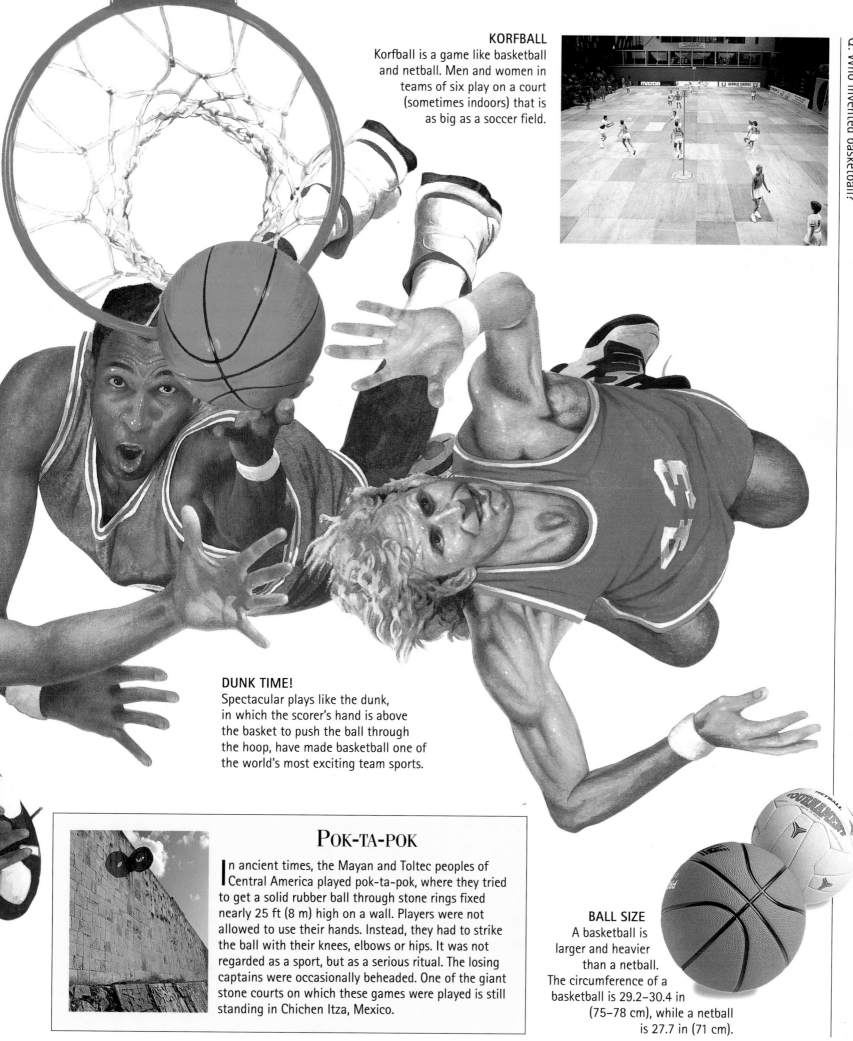

KORFBALL
Korfball is a game like basketball and netball. Men and women in teams of six play on a court (sometimes indoors) that is as big as a soccer field.

DUNK TIME!
Spectacular plays like the dunk, in which the scorer's hand is above the basket to push the ball through the hoop, have made basketball one of the world's most exciting team sports.

POK-TA-POK
In ancient times, the Mayan and Toltec peoples of Central America played pok-ta-pok, where they tried to get a solid rubber ball through stone rings fixed nearly 25 ft (8 m) high on a wall. Players were not allowed to use their hands. Instead, they had to strike the ball with their knees, elbows or hips. It was not regarded as a sport, but as a serious ritual. The losing captains were occasionally beheaded. One of the giant stone courts on which these games were played is still standing in Chichen Itza, Mexico.

BALL SIZE
A basketball is larger and heavier than a netball. The circumference of a basketball is 29.2–30.4 in (75–78 cm), while a netball is 27.7 in (71 cm).

17

THE FIELD
The standard soccer field is 328–387 ft (100–118 m) long and 210–240 ft (64–73 m) wide. A line about 54 ft (16.5 m) from each goal marks the penalty area. If a defender commits a foul in this area, the other side is awarded a penalty kick.

HEADS UP
Soccer players use their heads as well as their feet to control the ball, to pass it or to score goals. They are not allowed to touch it with their hands.

Soccer

Soccer, or association football as it was originally called, is the world's most popular code of football. Most ancient cultures, including the Chinese and Romans, played a game that involved kicking a ball-like object. The Vikings used the heads of their enemies, others used animal bladders or bundles of cloth. In the 1800s, different forms of the game were played at schools and universities. In 1848, a code of rules was drawn up at Cambridge University in England. The Football Association was formed in England in 1863. Soccer is a highly skillful team game with 11 players on each side. The object of the game is to score by getting the ball into the opposition's goal. Players can use their feet, thighs, chest, head—any part of their body except for their arms or hands—to control or strike the ball.

STRANGE BUT TRUE
Archaeologists have unearthed many clues to show that ancient civilizations played a round-ball version of football. Among the objects found in an Egyptian pharaoh's tomb was this ball, which is now on display at the British Museum.

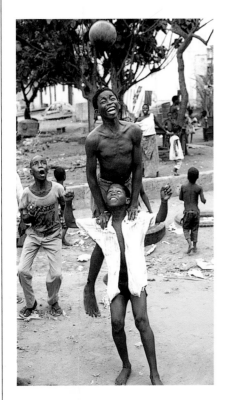

STREET BEAT
Young soccer enthusiasts all over the world play street soccer. Many soccer champions started their careers on their neighborhood streets.

SCISSOR LEGS
In the scissor kick, the player lifts off the ground and kicks the ball back over his head. Although spectacular goals have been scored using this kick, it is not tried very often because it is hard to do successfully.

A RUGBY SCRUM
In the scrum, the opposing sets of forwards work in formation to try to push each other out of position as they battle for the ball by rucking (hooking) it back with their feet.

BONUS KICK
After a try is scored, the team is allowed a free kick for goal. The ball must pass over the crossbar and between the uprights. If it does, it is called a conversion.

Rugby

Rugby union and rugby league are two codes of football that developed from a game played in the early 1800s at the famous Rugby School in England. The game became popular in other schools and colleges and eventually spread throughout the world. Rugby was played mainly by "gentlemen" and members of the upper classes in the southern counties of England. It was an amateur sport–the players did not receive any money for playing matches. But players in the working areas of northern England demanded expenses to cover their loss of wages. As this changed their amateur status, they formed a separate group, which in 1895 was called the Northern Union. This breakaway group changed the rules of the game and called their new sport "rugby league." The main difference between the two rugbys is that league has 13 players per team and union has 15 players.

BATTLE FOR THE BALL
When the rugby union ball goes out of play, the game restarts with a line-out. The opposing forwards from each team leap high in an attempt to claim the ball as it is thrown back into play by the hooker.

American Football

The most popular style of football played in the United States is American football. Based on a combination of the rules of rugby and soccer, American football developed in schools and universities during the 1860s. Walter Camp drafted the rules of the American football code in 1876, and the new sport soon became the nation's favorite winter game. It is a team sport with 11 players on each side. To score points, players must carry the ball or receive it over their opponents' goal line for a touchdown, or kick the ball through the upright goal posts for either a field goal or a conversion after a touchdown. University or college football attracts big crowds and is shown on television. The main professional organization is the National Football League (NFL) which began as the American Football Association in 1920. Today, the member clubs are multimillion-dollar business enterprises. They pay their players high salaries in an attempt to win the NFL championship.

THE SPECIALIST
Although there are only 11 players on each side at a time, as many as 40 may be used in a single game. They include specialist players such as the punt kicker who is called into play to kick the ball downfield.

THE GRIDIRON
The playing field is sometimes called the gridiron because it resembles the wire rack used for grilling food. It is 360 ft (110 m) long and 160 ft (49 m) wide. The field is divided into "yard lines," each about 15 ft (4.6 m) apart.

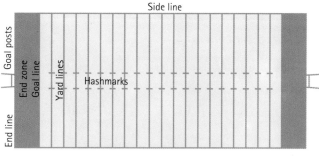

Side line

Goal posts
End zone
Goal line
Yard lines
Hashmarks
End line

FACE TO FACE
The teams face each other along an imaginary line called the line of scrimmage. After play begins, the defenders try to tackle the ball-carrier while his team-mates attempt to block them so the ball-carrier can run or pass.

MIXED BUSINESS
Because soccer is a game based on skill rather than strength, girls can play in mixed competitions with boys. When they are older, however, girls and boys usually choose to play in separate leagues.

THE WORLD GAME
By the early twentieth century, soccer was played in Europe and South America. Today, it is played in approximately 200 countries.

THE WORLD CUP

Soccer-playing nations compete every four years in the World Cup tournament to decide the world championship. Almost 170 countries enter the tournament and play in a series of elimination matches to decide which teams will qualify for the finals. Like the Olympic Games, it is a great honor for a nation to host the finals. The first World Cup finals tournament was held in 1930 in Uruguay. The home team defeated Argentina 4–2. Brazil, pictured here after winning the 1994 final, has been the most successful nation in the history of the World Cup.

SAVING A GOAL
The only player on the field allowed to handle the ball is the goalkeeper, but he must remain in the zone known as the penalty area. Here, the striker has beaten the tackler, but has not been able to get the ball past the goalkeeper to score a goal.

TRY TIME!

The objective in both rugby league and rugby union is to get the ball over the goal line for a try. The defending team tries to tackle the ball-carrier, usually around the legs, to prevent him from scoring the try.

THE HISTORY OF RUGBY

Legend has it that in 1823, William Webb Ellis, a student at Rugby School in England, broke the rules of soccer by picking up the ball and running with it. Word spread of Ellis's daring feat and soon others were doing the same. Some called this new sport the "running game," but to others it was known as the game played at Rugby. In time, this new code of football was called rugby. A plaque at the school records Ellis's role in history. Today, the teams of the rugby-playing nations, including the South African Springboks, New Zealand All Blacks and Australian Wallabies, compete every four years for the World Cup. This is also called the Webb Ellis Cup to honor the boy who supposedly first ran with the ball.

THE RUGBY FIELD

The fields for rugby union and rugby league are almost identical—no more than 328 ft (100 m) long and 223 ft (68 m) wide. This diagram shows a basic field. Lines are changed depending on which game is being played.

Dead ball line
Goal line
Goal posts
Halfway line
In-goal area
Touch line

POWER AND SPEED
American football is a very physical, body-contact game that involves blocking, tackling, running and passing the ball. Players at the top level need to be very fast and strong.

THE SUPER BOWL

The annual Super Bowl game to decide the NFL championship was introduced in 1967. It is one of the biggest events in American sports and is watched by millions of television viewers around the world, including people who may not even understand the rules of the game. They enjoy watching the entertainment program before the kick-off and during breaks in the game. This tradition started at college games with cheerleading squads and marching bands, but has since become a major form of sports entertainment.

BOWLING STYLES

There are two main methods of bowling—fast and slow. A slow bowler often spins the ball so that it bounces off the pitch in an unexpected direction. A fast bowler delivers the ball at a very high speed.

Slow bowling
The slow bowler has a short follow-through.

Fast bowling
The fast bowler has a much longer follow-through.

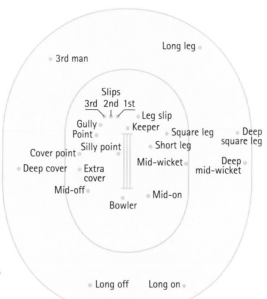

Long leg
3rd man
Slips
3rd 2nd 1st
Leg slip
Gully
Point
Keeper
Square leg
Deep square leg
Cover point
Silly point
Short leg
Deep cover
Extra cover
Mid-wicket
Deep mid-wicket
Mid-off
Mid-on
Long off
Long on
Bowler

IN THE FIELD

Cricket is played on an oval field that has a pitch 66 ft (20 m) long in the middle. The members of the fielding team are usually placed at any of the marked fielding positions to catch or stop the ball.

BAT AND BALL

The standard cricket bat is made of wood with a rubber grip. The ball is hard with an outer coating of red leather stitched into a seam.

• BAT AND BALL •

Cricket

For centuries, the traditional game of cricket has been a part of village life throughout England. For the last 100 years, it has been played as an international sport by countries that were once colonized by the British. Although King Edward I of England mentioned cricket as early as 1300, nobody really knows how the sport began. The cricket bat of 350 years ago looked more like a hockey stick, and the ball was bowled along the ground. Instead of three stumps, there were two. As the ball often rolled between the two stumps when bowlers tried to hit them, a third stump was added. In the 1800s, the modern style of overarm bowling became popular. Cricket is played between two teams of 11 players. The batting team has two players on the field trying to score runs, while the fielding team (all 11 players) tries to get them out.

IN THE STREET

Children around the cricketing world have long played a street version of the sport with their own rules for batting, bowling and fielding.

26

WOMEN AT THE WICKET

Although more men play the game, cricket has long been popular with women. At first, it was mainly a social sport, but today, women cricketers play for their country in the World Cup.

STUMPED!

The batsman dives in vain to make it back into the safety of the crease (the lined area). He is too late—the wicketkeeper takes the ball in his glove and removes the bails to complete the stumping. This is one of the ways that a batsman can be out.

THE ASHES

The most famous cricket trophy, the Ashes, sits just 4 in (10.6 cm) high on its stand. It is the prize for the victors in a series of matches, called test matches, between England and Australia. The trophy was created in 1882 after Australia's first win over England. Some people said this moment marked the death of English cricket. A humorous death notice was put in a London newspaper saying, "The body will be cremated and the ashes taken to Australia." A bail or a stump (it is not certain which) was later burned and its ashes were placed in the tiny urn.

DID YOU KNOW?

In the history of international cricket, there have been only two tied test matches. The first was in 1960 when Australia played the West Indies in Brisbane, Australia, and the other was in 1986 when India played Australia in Madras, India.

Baseball

Baseball is the national sport of the United States. It is also played in most parts of the world, and is especially popular in the Caribbean, Latin America and Japan. The game is believed to be based on rounders, a sport that flourished in England during the nineteenth century. Baseball is played on a diamond-shaped field with two teams of nine players. The aim of the game is to score more runs than the other team. A run is scored when a batter hits the ball thrown by the pitcher and completes a full circuit of the four bases. Batters can do this by stopping at any of the bases on the way, or by hitting the ball so far that they can complete the circuit without stopping. This is called a home run or a homer. One team bats while the other team fields. Both teams receive nine turns to bat, each of which is known as an inning.

Baseball

Softball

T-ball

BATS AND BALLS
The standard baseball bat is usually heavier and wider than the softball bat. The T-ball bat is ideal for small children. Notice how much smaller the hard baseball is when compared to the softball.

SITTING TARGET
T-ball is a modified version of baseball. Instead of the ball being thrown by the pitcher, it is placed on a stand. This makes it easy for the batter to hit.

SLIDE RULE
The batter races against the ball as he slides into the base. If the opposing player gets the ball and steps on the base or tags the runner before he reaches the base, the runner is out.

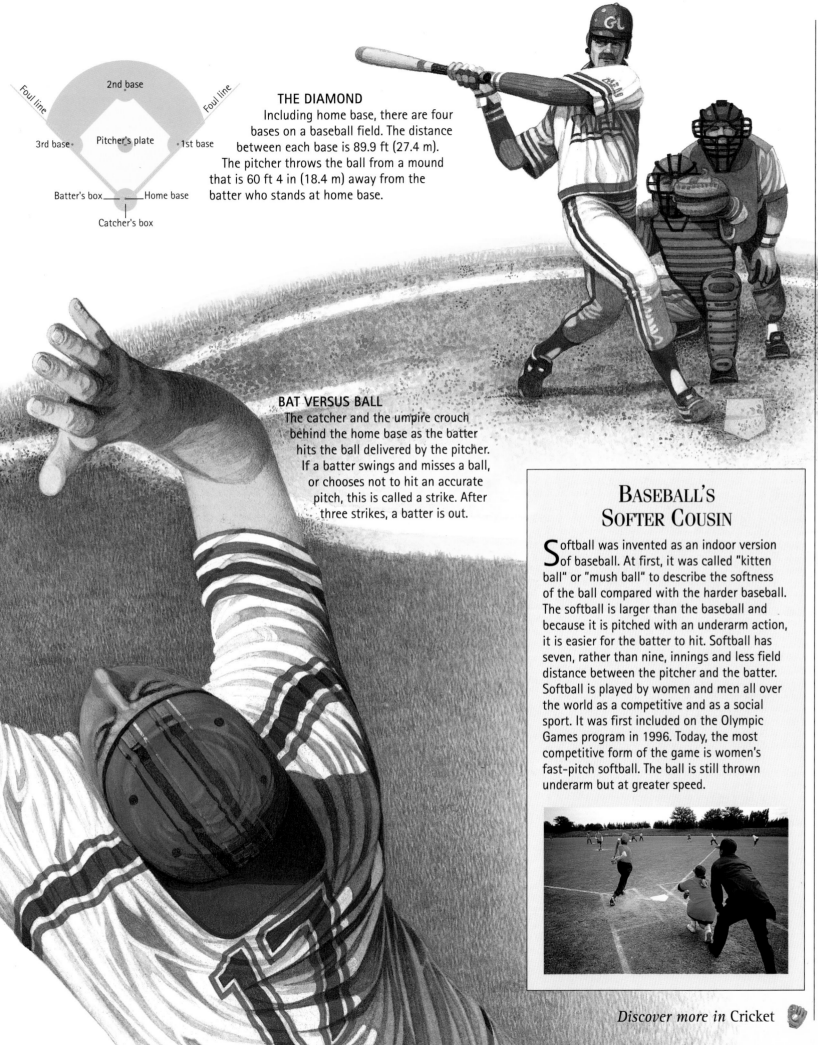

THE DIAMOND

Including home base, there are four bases on a baseball field. The distance between each base is 89.9 ft (27.4 m). The pitcher throws the ball from a mound that is 60 ft 4 in (18.4 m) away from the batter who stands at home base.

2nd base

Foul line
Foul line

3rd base · · Pitcher's plate · 1st base

Batter's box — Home base

Catcher's box

BAT VERSUS BALL

The catcher and the umpire crouch behind the home base as the batter hits the ball delivered by the pitcher. If a batter swings and misses a ball, or chooses not to hit an accurate pitch, this is called a strike. After three strikes, a batter is out.

BASEBALL'S SOFTER COUSIN

Softball was invented as an indoor version of baseball. At first, it was called "kitten ball" or "mush ball" to describe the softness of the ball compared with the harder baseball. The softball is larger than the baseball and because it is pitched with an underarm action, it is easier for the batter to hit. Softball has seven, rather than nine, innings and less field distance between the pitcher and the batter. Softball is played by women and men all over the world as a competitive and as a social sport. It was first included on the Olympic Games program in 1996. Today, the most competitive form of the game is women's fast-pitch softball. The ball is still thrown underarm but at greater speed.

Discover more in Cricket

• ON TARGET •

Golf

A DRIVING SHOT
The player "tees off" for the first shot by pushing the tee into the ground, placing the ball on it and then striking the ball, usually with a wooden-headed club known as a driver.

No-one really knows how golf began. Some have suggested that the first golfer was a shepherd in Scotland who hit stones with his hooked stick (called a crook). When he accidentally hit a stone into a rabbit hole, he began to take turns with a friend to see who was better at hitting stones into the hole! Many other cultures, such as Chinese, Celtic and Dutch, played games that were similar to modern golf. The aim of golf is to hit the ball from a starting point, known as the tee, into the hole on the green in the least number of shots. A round of golf is played over nine or 18 holes and the player who finishes with the fewest shots is declared the winner. The first golf balls were made of wood and the first clubs were tree branches. Later, club makers added separate heads made of wood, iron and steel. The rubber-core ball was introduced in the twentieth century.

THE BIRTH OF GOLF
St. Andrews in Scotland is the birthplace of modern golf. The club built on this course, the Royal and Ancient Club, laid down the first rules of the game. The British Open, one of the world's great tournaments, has often been held on this course.

TRAPS FOR THE UNWARY
Golf courses include hazards such as sand traps, or bunkers. If a ball lands in a bunker, it is difficult for the golfer to play a good shot out of the sand.

CADDIES
The word caddie comes from the French word "cadet" meaning a "little chief." In ancient Scotland it was used to describe pageboys or messengers. In time, boys who carried and cleaned the sticks of wealthy golfers were called caddies. Today, motorized carts are common on most golf courses, but caddies still carry the bags of the top players in tournament golf. They have a great knowledge of the game and their advice is highly valued by professional golfers.

BASIC EQUIPMENT
Golf bags are used to carry clubs, balls and tees. Clubs have different names and each is used for a different type of shot.

Putter
A putter is used for tapping, or putting, the ball into the hole.

Iron
An iron is used for medium-range shots.

Wood
A wood or driver is used for long shots from the tee.

Discover more in Billiards, Pool and Snooker

Bowls and Bowling

The Romans introduced the game of bowls to the northern European countries we now know as France, Germany and Britain. The Italians still play this game, called bocce, with only minor differences. The aim of most forms of bowls is to toss or roll the bowl or bowls near to the target bowl, which is called the jack. The winning player or team is the one that rolls the greatest number of bowls nearest the jack. The game can be played between single players or teams of two to four players. Lawn bowling is played on flat greens, but in crown green bowling the lawn slopes gently up to the center, or crown, of the green. Indoor, or carpet bowls, is very similar to lawn bowling but it is played indoors on a carpet or synthetic green. The most famous bowler in history was the English sailor Sir Francis Drake. Legend says that in 1588, he refused to fight the warships of the invading Spanish Armada until he had finished his game of bowls.

PLAYING BOWLS

By the nineteenth century, variations on the game of bowls were played throughout Europe. The Italians enjoyed bocce, the English played lawn bowling and the French liked to relax with a game of boules, or pétanque, such as the one being played here.

CURLERS AND SOOPERS

Players in the game of curling slide a stone on the ice from one target area to another that is 112 ft (34 m) away. Sweepers called soopers sweep the ice in front of the stone with brooms to remove any objects in its path and to help it travel faster.

MARBLES

The game of marbles is similar to bowls. Its players are rewarded for hitting the jack or knocking an opponent's marble out of the way.

DIFFERENT BALLS

The tenpin bowling ball can weigh up to 16 lb (7.2 kg). A lawn ball weighs up to 3 lb 8 oz (1.59 kg), and a boules ball weighs only 2 lb 3 oz (1 kg).

Tenpin ball

Lawn ball

Boules ball

BIASED BOWLS

The bias on a bowling ball makes it swerve to one side. Here, lawn bowlers roll the ball on a curved path to get closer to the jack.

PINS, STRIKES AND ALLEYS

In tenpin bowling, a large ball is rolled down a wooden alley in an attempt to knock down a set of pins set up in a triangular formation. The original tenpin bowling alley was a church aisle and the game was played by European churchmen. It was introduced to the United States by the Dutch in the seventeenth century. It became very popular in the 1950s when the automatic pinsetter was invented. This replaced the fallen pins in the correct positions ready for the next bowler. Knocking down all the pins with one bowl is known as a strike.

Chalk
Players rub chalk on the end of the cue to prevent it from sliding on the cue ball.

Curved rest
Players reach the cue ball safely by placing a curved rest over a ball that is in the way.

Crosspiece rest
Players can rest the cue on the crosspiece if the cue ball is out of their reach.

The cue
A standard cue is a tapered stick that must not be less than 3 ft (95 cm) long.

The bridge
Players spread their hand and use their thumb and index finger to guide them when they play a shot.

IN THE STREETS
Croquet grew from an old game called pall mall, where people used a mallet to drive a ball through iron rings placed at various distances along an alley or street. One famous London street where the game was popular was later renamed Pall Mall.

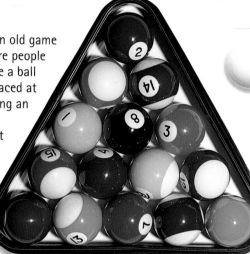

Cue ball

SETTING UP
At the start of a game of pool, the players place 15 balls inside a frame in a triangular formation. They remove the frame and play the first shot of the match by striking this formation with the white cue ball.

• ON TARGET •

Billiards, Pool and Snooker

EYEING THE BALL
Snooker was invented in India in 1875 by British army officers who wanted a more exciting version of billiards. Today, professional snooker players earn huge prize money in televised tournaments, including the World Championship.

Billiards is thought to have started when bad weather drove avid bowlers and croquet players indoors. In the beginning, players used a wooden pole to move the ball across the floor. Later, the pole was replaced by a tapered stick called a cue and the game was played on an elevated platform or table covered in green cloth to represent lawn. From billiards, the games of snooker and then pool developed. By the 1940s, these two games became more popular than billiards. Billiards is played with three balls, one red and two white. Snooker is played with 15 red balls, six balls in other colors and one white cue ball. Pool, also called pocket billiards, has a white cue ball and 15 numbered, colored balls. Today, all three games are played on a rectangular table that has pockets in the corners and sides. Points are scored by knocking the balls into the pockets with the cue ball.

34

PLAYING THE SHOTS

A billiards player can score points by sinking one of the three balls, as the player here is attempting, or by playing a "cannon." The cannon occurs when the cue ball hits the other two balls in succession. When a ball is sunk in a pocket, it is returned to the table for further play.

THE RISE AND FALL OF CROQUET

By the beginning of the eighteenth century, the sport of pall mall had nearly disappeared. By the 1850s it was back under the new name of croquet. At first the game was popular in France and Ireland. It soon spread to England where rules were drawn up in the 1860s and the All England Croquet Club was formed in 1868. Croquet, a gentle game of skill rather than vigor, was played by people of all ages. Since the beginning of the twentieth century, however, the number of croquet players and greens has fallen dramatically.

PLAYING POOL

In the game of pool, the balls numbered from one to eight are plain colored. The balls numbered from nine to fifteen are striped. The number eight ball (colored black) must be sunk last.

Archery and Darts

Before the invention of gunpowder, bows and arrows were the main weapons used in Europe in the Middle Ages. Legends were created about the skill of famous archers, such as Robin Hood. When armies replaced their bows and arrows with firearms, archery was practiced mainly as a sport. There are two types of archery—target and field. In target archery, the archers shoot at a fixed target. Field archery takes place in forests or on open ground, with targets of different sizes set at various distances. In both, the aim is to score points by firing arrows as closely as possible to the center of the target. The innermost circle of the target is known as the bull's-eye. Archery contests can take place at indoor and outdoor ranges, and since 1931, world championships have been held every two years. Archery is also featured on the Olympic Games program.

IN FLIGHT
Arrows have a vane—a tail of feathers or plastic—to help them fly better. They are usually tipped with points so that they will stick into the target.

BOWS
Most bows are made out of carbon or wood. The powerful compound bow is used for field archery, while the recurve bow can be used for both field and target competition.

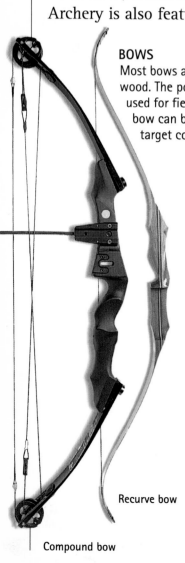

Recurve bow

Compound bow

A TEST OF ACCURACY
Modern archers practice the same basic skills as their ancestors of hundreds of years ago. Here, an archer is taking part in target archery, the most common form of competition archery.

SOCIAL SCENE
Although bows and arrows were no longer weapons of war in nineteenth-century Europe, archery was enjoyed by both men and women as a competitive and social sport.

DID YOU KNOW?
Anne Boleyn the second wife of Henry VIII of England, gave him a set of jewel-encrusted darts as a birthday present.

THREE DARTS AND A BOARD
Darts can be traced back to fifteenth-century England where the game was introduced as an indoor activity. It is played with three weighted metal darts each about 5 in (14 cm) long. The darts are thrown at a board 1 ft 6 in (45.7 cm) in diameter. The player throwing the dart stands 8 ft 10 in (2.7 m) from the board. There are many ways to play darts, and one of the most popular methods of scoring is to start with a certain number and to keep subtracting the points scored. The winner is the first player to reach zero.

SMALLER SHOTS
Like archery, the popular indoor game of darts is also a test of accuracy. Instead of using a bow to fire the darts at the target, players simply throw them at the dartboard.

WINNING HOLDS

In an amateur wrestling match, points are scored for pinning an opponent to the mat, keeping him in a hold, or escaping from a hold. A freestyle wrestling match is won by a number of techniques, including pinfalls, knockouts or submissions.

Outside ankle pick
The weight of his opponent and the upward pressure on his ankle pins the fallen wrestler to the mat.

Leg and arm lock
By using his body weight and a grip on both leg and arm, a wrestler attempts to pin his opponent.

Fireman's carry
One wrestler has exerted his superior strength and skill by lifting his opponent off the mat.

THE REFEREE

In a tournament match, the referee wears a red band on one arm and a blue band on the other to signify the colors of each contestant.

Wrestling

Wrestling is the oldest known competitive sport. Greeks and Romans included wrestling in festivals such as the ancient Olympic Games. Native Americans, Chinese, Mongolians and Japanese all had their own forms of wrestling. They all involved two unarmed opponents who tried to secure a fall by means of a body grip, strength or skill. Many different forms of wrestling are practiced today. In Greco-Roman wrestling, holds are limited to above the waist, and legs and feet cannot be used to trip an opponent. In freestyle wrestling, there are fewer restrictions on the number of holds used. Both freestyle and Greco-Roman wrestling are Olympic sports with contestants taking part in a series of elimination rounds. Wrestlers compete against opponents of similar weight. The weight limit for a light flyweight (the lightest division) is 106 lb (48 kg). The limit for the giants of the super heavyweight division is 286 lb (130 kg). Professional wrestling uses the freestyle form but is considered more of an entertainment than a sport.

AN ARTIST'S VIEW

Wrestling was very popular in ancient societies such as Greece, Rome and Egypt. Many works of art that have survived from these times show figures wrestling.

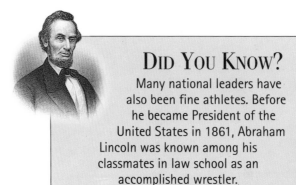

DID YOU KNOW?

Many national leaders have also been fine athletes. Before he became President of the United States in 1861, Abraham Lincoln was known among his classmates in law school as an accomplished wrestler.

SUMO SURVIVES

In modern Japan, the ancient art of sumo wrestling, which was once part of the samurai warrior's training, is more popular than ever. Each sumo wrestler attempts to score a fall by moving his opponent, who may weigh more than 442 lb (200 kg), from the wrestling ring.

WRESTLING DRESS

In yagli, a Turkish form of wrestling, competitors smear themselves with grease to make it difficult for opponents to grip them. Russian jacket wrestlers use each other's clothing to apply a grip, while Japanese sumo wrestlers are permitted to take hold of each other's belt. In the Middle East, where a belt was once a sign of a person's importance, the entire contest involved the wrestlers gripping each other's belt in their efforts to force a fall. The Greek bronze statuette (above), which is from the fourth century BC, shows naked (and probably greased) wrestlers.

Blue corner
Passivity zone
Center
Protection zone
Red corner

IN THE RING

Wrestling contests are held on a mat at least 1.6 in (4 cm) thick within a circle 29 ft 6 in (9 m) in diameter. The red circle, called the passivity zone, warns the wrestlers they are near the edge of the mat. One corner is marked in red and one in blue to signify the color of the singlet worn by each wrestler.

JUDO
In a judo bout, contestants are judged on their ability to throw an opponent to the floor. This technique is known in Japanese as "nagewaza."

• BODY SKILLS •

Martial Arts and Fencing

Many centuries ago, people in Asia combined physical exercise with the art of self-defense. This form of training is known as martial arts, and it includes ju-jitsu, kendo and tae kwon do. Judo, which in Japanese means "the gentle way" because it uses as little force as possible, developed from ju-jitsu and was accepted as an Olympic sport in 1964. Contestants use throws, locks and holds to force their opponent to submit. In self-defense karate, fighters kick and strike each other with their hands, knees and elbows. In competition karate, actual blows are not allowed. The word "karate" means "empty hand" in Japanese because the sport does not use any weapons. Fencing, or the sport of sword fighting, is another ancient military skill. It has been part of the Olympics since the first modern games in 1896. Swords were eventually replaced by specially made fencing items such as the foil, épée and light fencing saber.

FENCING EQUIPMENT
All fencing weapons today have a flexible steel blade. With the foil and the épée, a hit is scored with the point. With the saber, the point and cutting edge can be used. A protective mask and a glove must be worn.

Protective mask

Saber

Epée

Glove

Foil

TAE KWON DO
Blocking, punching and parrying are used in tae kwon do, but this popular form of hard-contact martial arts is best known for its range of kicking techniques.

A FLYING KICK

Kicks, blows and punches are all scoring techniques in the competitive combat sport of karate. In competition, fighters pull back their blows before they make contact with their opponents to prevent injuring them. Because karate developed from a form of self-defense designed to stop an attacker, many karate techniques are too dangerous to be used in competition. Contestants score points by using correct karate methods on the scoring parts of an opponent's body. A fighter who uses excessive physical force is disqualified.

ON GUARD!
For French musketeers of the seventeenth century, dueling with swords was not just a popular sport. Sometimes they fenced to settle a disagreement, or defend their honor. Swordsmen were often injured or died in these contests.

PARALYMPICS

Every four years, the best athletes with a disability from around the world compete at the Paralympics. In the track program, athletes in wheelchairs take part in sprint, middle-distance and long-distance events.

THROWING THE DISC

Competitors in the discus event try to throw a wooden disc edged in metal the longest distance. They must make their throw from inside a circle 8 ft 2 in (2.5 m) across.

• BODY SKILLS •

Track and Field

Foot races held in Greece thousands of years ago were probably the first organized athletics. Today, running, walking, jumping and throwing are all part of the world of track and field. Both categories of events—track and field—demand a wide range of skills from contestants. At a championship meet, the track program is made up of sprint, middle-distance, distance, relay, hurdle and walking races. The field events include jumping competitions, such as the high and long jumps; and throwing events, such as the javelin, discus, hammer and shot put. The decathlon for men brings together many of the track and field skills in one competition made up of ten events. The heptathlon is a seven-event contest for women. The two most important track and field meets are the World Championships and the Olympic Games, both of which take place every four years.

GREAT LEAP

The high jump is a field event in which the competitor uses strength and agility to jump over the crossbar without dislodging it.

POINT FIRST

The javelin is a throwing event based on the skill of throwing a spear in hunting or warfare. The javelin must land point first and the winner is whoever can throw it the longest distance.

HURDLES

Hurdle events combine the two skills of running and jumping and are part of the track program at a track and field meet. If competitors knock over a hurdle, it slows them down but they are not penalized.

42

THE OLYMPICS

Track and field events formed the basic program for the ancient Olympics and are just as important to the modern Olympics. Held in the main Olympic stadium, the track and field program brings together the world's best athletes. After a series of heats and elimination contests, the finest performers are left to compete for the gold medals in the Olympic finals. Because athletes value an Olympic gold medal above all other sporting trophies, they train hard to be at the very peak of their performance for the games. Often, world records are broken during the finals as the track and field contestants strive to go higher, faster or farther. These events are watched by thousands of spectators in the Olympic stadium, and the pictures are beamed live around the world to billions of television viewers.

THE HORIZONTAL BAR

The horizontal bar is 9 ft (2.75 m) high and allows competitors to perform such exercises as swings and single-handed handstands. Great strength and control is required to perform on the bar. It is used only in men's competitions.

THE FLOOR

The floor routine is common to both men's and women's gymnastics. In women's competition, the gymnast must show dance steps as well as acrobatic and gymnastic elements in her routine.

Gymnastics

The Egyptians, Greeks, Chinese, Minoans, Etruscans and Romans all practiced acrobatics as a form of entertainment and a way to celebrate the fitness and flexibility of the human body. These acrobatic displays were the forerunners of competitive gymnastics. One of the pioneers of modern gymnastics was Friedrich Ludwig Jahn. In 1811, he created the first open-air gymnasium and introduced such devices as the parallel bars and rings. Gymnastics became very popular in Europe, and it was one of the first sports included on the program for the first modern Olympic Games in 1896. Gymnastics takes in many kinds of movement and dance. There are three separate forms of competitive gymnastics: artistic gymnastics, rhythmic gymnastics and sport acrobatics. Each discipline requires different types of equipment and styles of performance.

FINE BALANCE

The beam is one of four disciplines in women's artistic gymnastics. At 16 ft 5 in (5 m) long but just 4 in (10 cm) wide, the beam is a great test of the gymnast's balance and agility.

THE RINGS
The rings are one of six disciplines in men's artistic gymnastics. They hang 9 ft (2.75 m) above the floor and competitors perform handstands, swings and somersaults. Gymnasts need great strength and control to perform on the rings.

janssen/fritsen

TRAMPOLINING
Trampolining is an exhilarating form of exercise that developed from circus acrobatics. The trampoline is a webbed mat hung by springs from the sides of a frame set about 3 ft (1 m) above the floor. By jumping on the webbed mat, the trampoline gymnast gains great bounce from the springs. There are trampoline competitions for individuals, teams of five and synchronized pairs (pictured). Judges award marks for the difficulty of the exercises and the way they are performed. Marks are deducted for loss of height, breaks in the routine and loss of rhythm.

DID YOU KNOW?
The vaulting horse was developed from acrobatic routines practiced on real horses. When it was first used in Germany, the vaulting horse had a horse's head as well as a tail. Over the years, however, the horse lost its head and tail.

ACROBATIC SKILL
In this time-lapse photograph, the gymnast makes his run up to the springboard, performs a vault over the vaulting horse and completes a perfect landing on the other side.

Cycling

The sport of cycling is almost as old as the bicycle itself. Races were held on street courses until 1868 when the first recorded track race took place in Paris with competitors racing over 3,936 ft (1,200 m). Cycle tracks sprang up all over Europe, and by 1889 the top cyclists were being paid to race in front of large crowds. Great Britain was the most powerful cycling nation until 1900 when other European countries formed the Union Cycliste Internationale. There are two main types of competition racing: track racing and road racing. In track racing, cyclists race over sprint or longer distances on a banked circuit, or velodrome, which has curved, sloping sides. Road racing is held on public roads and may take many days and sometimes weeks to complete. During this time, the riders cover hundreds or even thousands of miles. Other types of bike racing are BMX (bicycle motocross), mountain-bike events and cyclo-cross, held over open country.

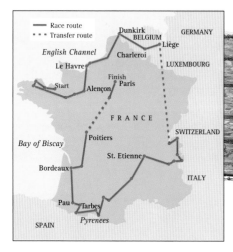

THE TOUR MAP
The route for the Tour de France can change each year. This was the route for 1995. However, the race always crosses the Pyrenees, where riders climb to heights of more than 8,200 ft (2,500 m), and it always finishes in Paris.

THE GREAT RACE
The most famous road race of all is the Tour de France. It is held over three weeks and covers more than 1,860 miles (3,000 km). People turn out to cheer the riders who come from all parts of the world. The leader at the end of each section has the honor of wearing a yellow jersey the next day.

DIFFERENT BIKES
The mountain bike has a strong frame for rough conditions and is fitted with brakes and gears. The road bike has brakes as well as a large selection of gears for hill climbing. The track bike has neither brakes nor gears.

Mountain bike

Road bike

Track bike

IN PURSUIT
A velodrome (right) is used for cycling events, such as the team pursuit (top). This race is held over 13,120 ft (4,000 m) between two teams that have four riders each. The winning team is decided by the finishing times of the first three riders of each team.

EARLY DAYS OF CYCLING

The invention of the chain-driven bicycle in the 1870s revolutionized this new means of transportation and enabled cyclists to travel at greater speeds. Cycling was soon recognized as a healthy form of exercise and a way to see the countryside. The Pickwick Cycle Club of London was the world's first club for people who wished to enjoy this new sport. Later, bicycle touring clubs were introduced to Europe and the rest of the world to promote the new pastime and to protect the rights of cyclists on the roads. Here, children in the Netherlands enjoy cycling on an extra large bicycle.

Backstroke

Breast stroke

SWIMMING CAP AND GOGGLES
A close-fitting cap helps streamline
the swimmer. Goggles protect the eyes
and make it easier to see underwater.

FLYING START
At the beginning of all
major swimming races,
except backstroke, the
competitors dive from
their starting blocks
into the water.

• IN THE SWIM •

Swimming and Diving

Swimming is one of the most popular sports in the world. The earliest swimming competition on record was held in Japan in 36 BC. Today, swimmers compete at all levels—from races held in school pools to long-distance swimmers battling the seas of the English Channel. The fastest and strongest swimmers in the world race against each other at the World Championships and the Olympic Games. In a pool that is 164 ft (50 m) long and divided into eight lanes, they usually swim either freestyle, butterfly, backstroke or breast stroke, though some specialize in more than one stroke. Races are set over distances of 164 ft (50 m) to 4,920 ft (1,500 m). Diving is also an Olympic sport and is separated into springboard and platform events. Divers perform a set number of dives, which are rated for their degree of difficulty. Judges award points on how well the dives are performed.

WATER POLO
Water polo
originated in
England and was
included on the
program of the
second modern
Olympics held in 1900.
It is a combination of
soccer and volleyball.
Water-polo players need
to be excellent swimmers.

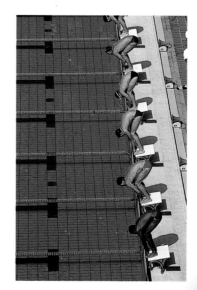

Freestyle

Butterfly

SWIMMING STROKES
Top-class swimmers usually specialize in one of the four swimming strokes. But some can swim all strokes very well. They compete in an event called the medley, which is made up of equal distances of each stroke.

WATER BALLET

Synchronized swimmers perform acrobatic and dancelike routines to music. They move with grace and rhythm, and judges award them marks for the quality of their movements in the water. Synchronized swimmers compete in solo, duet or team performances in a pool that is at least 10 ft (3 m) deep. It has underwater speakers so that performers can hear the music while they twist and turn under water. Australian Annette Kellermann and American Esther Williams are famous synchronized swimmers.

HIGH DIVER
In his dive from the 33-ft (10-m) platform, an international competitor displays the classic pike position—bent at the hips, feet together and toes pointed. He will enter the water with his arms extended in front of his head and his body in a straight line.

Discover more in Gymnastics

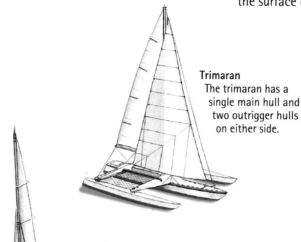

BODY-SURFING
Not all surfers need a board to catch a wave. A body-surfer swims onto the breaking wave and uses his body and hands to glide towards the shore.

SAILBOARDING
In wave sailing, sailboarders ride their boards up the face of a breaking wave and use it as a ramp to make spectacular aerial maneuvers high above the surface of the water.

Catamaran
The lightweight catamaran has twin hulls. It is a popular form of racing and leisure craft.

Trimaran
The trimaran has a single main hull and two outrigger hulls on either side.

SAILING CRAFT
There are many types of sailing craft, such as catamarans, trimarans and yachts.

Yacht
The keel, which is part of the yacht's single hull, gives the boat extra stability.

WIND POWER
Under the power of the wind, a fleet of racing skiffs sails around a marker buoy that forms part of the course. The skiffs are trying to complete the course in the shortest time.

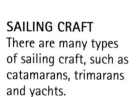

• IN THE SWIM •

Surfing and Sailing

The English explorer Captain James Cook saw people riding waves in their canoes when he was in the Polynesian islands in 1771. Eight years later, other visitors to the islands noted how the natives also lay on long, narrow surfboards as they rode the waves to the shore. Those boards were made of wood. Today's modern surfboards are crafted from foam and fiberglass and can be seen on beaches in such surfing locations as Australia, Hawaii, California, South Africa and some of the islands of Indonesia. A sailboard is like a surfboard with a mast and sail attached. Sailboarding can be performed in the surf or on still water. It is just one of more than 3,000 types of competitive sailing craft in the world. Whether on a tiny one-person dinghy or on a mighty maxi yacht with a crew of 24, sailing requires skill and experience.

IN THE TUBE
A surfer positions his board in the hollow part of the breaking wave known as the tube or the barrel. The tube ride is one of the highest scoring maneuvers in competitive surfing. By riding as close as possible to the breaking section, the surfer can gain maximum speed from the ride.

WATER-SKIING

A contestant in a slalom water-skiing competition throws a wall of spray as she banks through a tight turn. As a competitive sport, water-skiing involves jumping, slalom and trick riding. In jumping, skiers are judged on the length of the jump they make after skiing over a steep ramp with the boat traveling at a set speed. The slalom skiers must zigzag past six buoys in the fastest time. In the trick event, judges award points for tricks performed. Individual awards are made for each event, but the winner of the championship is the best skier over the three events.

SAFETY EQUIPMENT
White-water and slalom racing can be hazardous. Helmets protect paddlers from contact with rocks and other obstacles. Flotation devices prevent the craft from sinking.

DOWN RIVER
A two-person canoe heads down river. Its design is similar to a craft used by Native Americans thousands of years ago.

ESKIMO ROLL
Perhaps the most important safety technique a paddler must learn is the Eskimo roll. If a kayak capsizes, this maneuver allows the paddler to return to an upright position in seconds.

EIGHT PLUS ONE
The crews in the event known as the eights pull away from the start at a rowing regatta. The cox or coxswain, often the smallest crew member, sits in the stern to help keep the rowers on course and in perfect time.

DIFFERENT CRAFT
Both the canoe and the kayak are propelled by paddles and can be used in still-water and white-water competitions. The two craft, however, have some important differences, as shown.

Canoe
The canoe is an open boat with one, sometimes two, single-bladed paddles.

· IN THE SWIM ·

Rowing and Canoeing

People from the Stone Age hollowed out logs to make canoes, the Inuit (Eskimos) of North America stretched animal hides over frames to construct kayaks, and Polynesians of the Pacific Islands made outrigger canoes. These paddle-driven craft were among the most ancient forms of water transportation and were the forerunners of today's sports models, such as racing kayaks and Canadian class canoes. Olympic racing canoes are made of plywood but other models use fiberglass or aluminium. Kayak and canoe racing can take place on still water or white water, or over rapids. Rowing, which is held on still water, is also an Olympic sport. Sculling is a type of rowing, but the rower uses two oars (called sculls) instead of one. Rowing tournaments are called regattas and are held for crews of one, two, four or eight people. The most important rowing regattas are held at the World Championships and the Olympic Games.

Kayak
The kayak is an enclosed craft with a double-bladed paddle.

KAYAK RACING
Kayak racing over slalom and white-water courses tests the competitor's ability to control the craft in difficult conditions. In slalom racing, the kayak must pass through several gates set up over the course. A white-water racing course must be close to 2 miles (3 km) long.

DRAGON-BOAT RACES

Hundreds of paddles churn through the water to the sound of beating drums as the fearsome-looking craft in this dragon-boat race surge across Hong Kong Harbor. The most spectacular form of paddling craft, the dragon boats have 20 rowers, a crew member in the stern to steer and a drummer to help the paddlers keep time. Dragon-boat racing was originally part of an ancient Chinese festival. It has now been adopted by other countries and crews regularly take part in international competitions.

Q: What are the two main differences between a canoe and a kayak?

Helmet

Ski poles

Ski suit

Ski gloves

DOWNHILL DASH
Downhill skiing is a high-speed race against the clock. Competitors wear tight-fitting aerodynamic suits, and helmets to protect them in case they fall.

Ski boots

Skis

Skiing and Tobogganing

The people of the snow-covered lands of Scandinavia in northern Europe were the first people to ski. Thousands of years ago, they skied for practical reasons—to move around during winter—rather than for sport. Today, the sport of skiing falls into two main categories: nordic and alpine. Nordic includes cross-country, ski-jumping and biathlon, which consists of two events—skiing, and shooting at targets. Alpine takes in the faster events, such as slalom and downhill racing. As winter sports gained popularity, people soon adapted the sled and toboggan for racing. These had already been used for years to carry goods and passengers across snow and ice. The first bobsled races were held in Switzerland during the 1880s. Bobsled teams consist of two or four people racing a heavy sled down a high-speed, ice-walled track. The luge toboggan is built for one or two riders. Unlike the bobsled, it does not have brakes or a steering device.

TWISTING TURNS
Pairs of flags mark the course for the slalom skier. In a slalom race, skiers must complete the course twice. Their two recorded times are added together.

BOBBING ABOUT
The bobsled is made of steel with a lightweight body constructed of fiberglass or a composite material. The driver steers the bob with a rope attached to the front axle.

READY FOR TAKE-OFF
Distance, style and technique are all important as a ski jumper heads for the take-off point. This sport requires courage, grace and strength.

DANGEROUS DESCENT
Dressed in a helmet and aerodynamic suit, a luge rider hurtles feet first down a specially made course that is more than 3,280 ft (1,000 m) long. By moving his body, the competitor can apply pressure to the runners and steer the luge through the sloped curves of the course.

ACROBATIC SKIING

Freestyle skiing is the most modern form of this sport. It includes three events: ballet, moguls (a high-speed run over a bumpy course) and the spectacular aerials. Skiers in the aerials launch themselves off a steep ramp to perform twists, and single, double or even triple somersaults before attempting to land safely on a slope of soft snow. Skiers are awarded points for the quality of their take-offs, their style or form in the air, the height they reach and the accuracy of their landings. A snowboard (far left) allows its rider to perform maneuvers similar to those of surfboard riding.

Ice-skating

FIT FOR ROYALTY
This Royal Albert skate was made in the nineteenth century for Prince Albert of England. It featured an extended blade in the shape of a swan's head.

L ong before the days of the Vikings, the Norse people of northern Europe made ice skates from the shank (shin) bones of animals. They used staffs, or poles, to push themselves along the ice. Later, wood and eventually iron runners secured with straps replaced bone. Following the invention of refrigeration, the first artificially frozen indoor ice rink was opened in London in 1876. Today, there are two types of competitive skating: speed skating and figure skating. Both are Winter Olympic sports. In the speed events, competitors are judged not on their technique, but on their speed around a set course. Speed skaters compete over distances ranging from 1,640 ft (500 m) to 16,400 ft (5,000 m). A figure-skating championship meet is divided into men's, women's, ice-dancing and pairs competitions. A judging panel awards points for the way the skaters perform their routines.

SOCIAL SKATING
Skating has been a popular winter sport for a long time, as shown by this scene from a fifteenth-century Dutch woodcut.

ICE DANCING
Ice dancing is the most spectacular form of skating. It combines great artistic and athletic skill. The skaters perform a compulsory dance, an original dance and a free dance to accompanying music.

ICE RACING

With fingertips touching the ice to assist their balance, three speed skaters take a tight corner during a race at the 1994 Winter Olympics.

SKATING MANEUVERS

The single skater is judged on an original and a free-skating program. In the original program, each competitor performs eight compulsory maneuvers. Judges award two marks, one for the compulsory movements and one for the overall presentation. In the free-skating program, the skater chooses a number of movements such as jumps, spins and dance steps to perform with music. Judges award another two marks, one for technical ability and one for artistic expression. The skater placed first by a majority of judges is the winner.

FREE SKATING

The free-skating part of the pairs competition is considered one of the most challenging events. It allows the skaters to introduce their own moves and music, and to demonstrate their ability in all the main areas of skating, such as jumping and spinning.

Discover more in Gymnastics

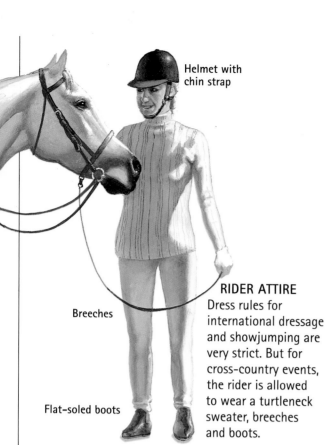

Helmet with chin strap

Breeches

Flat-soled boots

RIDER ATTIRE
Dress rules for international dressage and showjumping are very strict. But for cross-country events, the rider is allowed to wear a turtleneck sweater, breeches and boots.

SADDLES
Competitors in dressage events are required to use a kind of English hunting saddle. Show-jumpers, however, are allowed to use the saddle of their choice. The stock saddle shown here is a popular saddle for recreation and general use.

Horse Riding

Competition on horseback, or equestrian sport as it is known, dates almost from the time humans first learned to ride. The earliest recorded showjumping event, however, was held in Dublin, Ireland, in 1864. Today, in the Olympic Games, there are three types of equestrian event—dressage, cross-country and showjumping. The Olympic Games program also includes a three-day event, which is a contest of all three disciplines. Dressage is a competition in which the horse and rider perform a complicated set of maneuvers within a limited area. Showjumping is a contest in which the horse and rider must jump over a series of obstacles. The winner is the horse and rider with either the lowest number of faults or the fastest time. The cross-country event tests the speed, endurance and jumping ability of the horse over a long, open course.

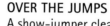

OVER THE JUMPS
A show-jumper clears an obstacle known as brush and rails. A typical international Grand Prix course would be made up of 15 jumps, including a water jump, triple vertical parallels, oil drums and poles, and a stone wall.

CROSS-COUNTRY
The aim of the cross-country event is to jump over the many obstacles on the course with as few mistakes as possible, and to keep within the time limit.

HARMONY OF HORSE AND RIDER
In international dressage, each competitor performs a routine including a number of paces (walk, canter and trot); halts; changes of direction; and figures, such as circles and figure eights. Their performance is judged by a jury of five officials.

THREE-DAY OLYMPIC EVENT

The three-day event is often the most exciting equestrian competition on the Olympic program. Held over three consecutive days, it includes dressage, cross-country and showjumping. It is run both as a team and an individual event. The team from each competing nation is made up of four members and the best three results are counted in the team's final score. At the same time, each member of the team is competing as an individual. Each rider must ride the same horse throughout the competition.

Q: What type of saddle is used in dressage events?

Sporting Personalities

Michael Jordan

After leading the University of North Carolina to the national college championship and the American team to the 1984 Olympic gold medal, basketball player Michael Jordan began his professional career with the Chicago Bulls. He carried the Bulls to three consecutive National Basketball Association (NBA) championships, and became the first basketball player to be named Most Valuable Player (MVP) in three straight NBA finals.

Carl Lewis

Born in 1961, American athlete Carl Lewis gained international fame with three victories at the 1983 World Championships. The following year he was awarded four gold medals in the 1984 Olympic Games. He won the long jump, the 100-m sprint, the 200-m sprint and the 4 x 100-m relay. Lewis competed at two more Olympic Games and won four more gold medals, including one for the 100-m sprint in 1988 when the winner, Ben Johnson, was disqualified for using drugs.

Carl Lewis

Pam Burridge

Surfing champion Pam Burridge from Sydney, Australia, won her first major title in 1979. During the next three years she was almost unbeatable, but later slipped from the top rankings because of strong competition. In 1990, however, she rediscovered her competitive drive to win the world crown.

Pam Burridge

Babe Ruth

George Herman (Babe) Ruth was born in 1895 and died in 1948. Until 1974 when his career record of 714 runs was bettered, he was the best home-run hitter of American baseball. Ruth had started as a pitcher with the Boston Red Sox in 1914, but soon discovered his true genius as a batter. He moved to the New York Yankees in 1920 and to the Boston Braves in 1934. In 1936, he was elected to the Baseball Hall of Fame.

Babe Ruth

Mark Spitz

Born in California, Mark Spitz was 22 years old when he emerged from the Munich Olympic pool in 1972 as the greatest swimmer in the history of the Olympic Games. He had won seven gold medals. From two Olympics, in 1968 and 1972, he earned a total of 18 medals—nine gold, five silver and four bronze.

Heather McKay

This Australian squash player won the world's leading championship, the British Open, a record 16 times. When world championships were contested in 1976 and 1979, McKay won both, the second after coming out of retirement at 40 years of age. From 1962 until her final tournament in 1979, she was undefeated.

Jack Nicklaus

American Jack Nicklaus is often acclaimed as the world's greatest golfer. Nicklaus, nicknamed "the Golden Bear," won the US Masters championship six times. He has also won five US Professional Golf Association championships, four US Open championships and three British Open championships.

Jack Nicklaus

60

Sir Donald Bradman

Cricket legend Don Bradman of Australia is the greatest batsman in the history of the game. In an international career that started in 1928 and ended in 1948, Bradman had a batting average of 99.94 runs. His average would have been more than 100 if he had not been dismissed for 0 in his final innings. No other player has come close to that record.

Joe Montana

A champion quarterback, Joe Montana won four Super Bowl championships with the San Francisco 49ers. In two of those finals he was selected as the Most Valuable Player (MVP). He was named the National Football League's (NFL) MVP on four occasions. He is the highest rated quarterback in NFL history.

Joe Montana

Sonja Henie

By the late 1920s, figure skating had been an international sport for 40 years, but it was not until Norway's Sonja Henie dazzled audiences that it became widely popular. Henie won gold medals at the 1928, 1932 and 1936 Winter Olympics, and her skill and artistry inspired generations of young skaters to take up the sport. After retiring as a skater, she became a Hollywood movie star.

Franz Klammer

In 1975, Austrian snow skier Franz Klammer won eight of nine World Cup downhill races. At the 1976 Winter Olympics in Innsbruck, Austria, he almost crashed several times at high speed in a desperate attempt to beat the fastest time set by defending

Martina Navratilova

champion Bernhard Russi of Switzerland. Klammer's courage and control gave him the gold medal by one-third of a second over Russi.

Martina Navratilova

Martina Navratilova was born in 1956 in Czechoslovakia and later became an American citizen. She was one of the world's outstanding tennis players of the 1970s and 1980s, and is one of the best of all time. She introduced a new level of power and fitness to women's tennis to win nine Wimbledon singles finals. Navratilova was named the 1980s athlete of the decade and became the highest paid player in the history of women's tennis.

Michael Chang

In 1987, at the age of 15 years and 6 months, Michael Chang became the youngest player to win a match in the main draw at the United States Open tennis championships. In 1988, he won his first Grand Slam tournament with a victory in the French Open. He is a sporting hero throughout Asia where he has won many tournaments.

Fanny Blankers-Koen

Fanny Blankers-Koen was 18 years old when she ran at the 1936 Olympics. Although she was the holder of six world records at the time of the 1948 Olympics, the Dutch champion was thought to be too old to compete. She went on to win four of the nine women's track and field events in the program.

Roger Bannister

On May 6, 1954, England's Roger Bannister became the first person to run the mile in less than four minutes. He used another runner to set the pace for him through the first half of the race. Bannister set a new world record of 3 minutes 59.4 seconds.

Pelé

Pelé

Legendary soccer player Edson Arantes do Nascimento, known to the fans as Pelé, led Brazil to three World Cup victories in 1958, 1962 and 1970. Still regarded as the greatest soccer player of all time, Pelé scored more than 1,000 goals and starred with the Santos club in Brazil before joining the New York Cosmos to help promote soccer in the United States.

Franz Klammer

Glossary

amateur A player who does not receive any payment for playing a sport.

backhand A stroke used in racket sports, such as tennis, squash and badminton, and played with the back of the hand turned towards the ball.

bails Two small wooden crosspieces set on top of the stumps in a game of cricket. In many cases, the bails have to be knocked from the stumps for the batsman to be dismissed.

bases The four fixed contact points a baseball batter must run to and touch on the way to scoring a run.

bias The curve of a bowling ball that is weighted on one side. The bowl usually rolls in an arc rather than a straight line.

catcher The person who, in baseball and softball, crouches behind the batter at home base and catches any balls missed by the batter.

court An enclosed area, or one specially marked out for a game. Games played on a court include tennis, croquet, basketball, netball and squash.

cox or coxswain A small, lightweight member of a rowing crew whose job is to keep the rowers in time and to steer the craft.

creases In cricket, these are the lines marked on the ground near each wicket that mark the playing positions for the batsman and the bowler.

cue ball In billiards, snooker and pool, the cue ball is the white ball. It is struck by the cue to make contact with the other balls.

decathlon An athletics contest of ten different events taking place over two days. On the first day, the individual must compete in the 100-m race, long jump, shot put, high jump and 400-m race. The second day includes the 110-m hurdles, discus, pole vault, javelin and 1500-m race.

diamond This refers to the marking of a baseball field, which looks like the outline of a diamond.

dribbling The process of moving the ball forwards with slight touches of hands, feet or sticks. Basketball, soccer and field-hockey players all dribble the ball.

elimination match A competition match in which the losing players leave the competition at the end of each round, until only the winner remains.

forehand A stroke played in racket sports with the palm of the hand turned towards the ball.

goalkeeper or goal-tender In soccer, field hockey and ice hockey, this person has the task of defending the goals to prevent the ball or puck from passing between the posts.

goals In some ball sports, the goals are special areas at which you aim the ball to score points. In various codes of football and hockey, the goal is a pair of posts through which a ball or puck is kicked or struck. In basketball and netball, it is a ring through which the ball is thrown.

Greco-Roman A style of wrestling in which you use the upper body but not the legs.

green In golf, this is the smooth putting area in which the hole is cut. In lawn bowling, it is the section of lawn used for a game.

heptathlon A track and field competition of seven separate events. On the first day, the individual must compete in the 100-m hurdles, high jump, shot put and 200-m race. The second day includes the long jump, javelin and 800-m race.

hippodrome A course used by ancient Greeks and Romans for the staging of chariot and horse races.

hoplite race A foot race held at the ancient Olympic Games. The competitors had to run naked except for helmets and leg armor, and carry their shields.

innings A team's turn at batting in cricket, softball, baseball and rounders.

jack The small white ball that players try to hit in the game of bowls.

javelin A light spear thrown by a competitor in a track and field event.

keel The lowest part of a sailing boat. It is often lined with lead or other heavy material to weight the boat and help keep it upright.

parallel bars Two bars of equal length supported by uprights used in gymnastic performances.

Paralympics An international sporting festival for athletes with a disability. Like the Olympic Games, the festival is held every four years.

Bowls, or bowling balls

Fireman's carry

Trimaran

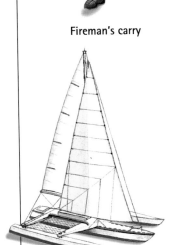
Fencing equipment

Badminton rackets and shuttlecock

pitch A marked playing area, such as a soccer or hockey field, and the area used for bowling and batting in a game of cricket. Pitch also means to throw or fling a ball, such as in baseball.

pitcher The player in a baseball or softball game whose task is to throw the ball at the batters. The pitcher is often regarded as the most valuable member of the team.

pok-ta-pok A game, similar to basketball, played in the tenth century BC by the Mayan and Toltec peoples of Central America.

professional An athlete or sporting person who competes for prize money or receives payment for playing a chosen sport.

puck A rubber disk used in ice hockey.

punt A type of football kick in which the kicker drops the ball from the hands. The kicker strikes the ball with the foot before the ball touches the ground.

racket A wooden, metal or synthetic bat strung with nylon or other material. It is used to hit the ball in such sports as tennis, squash and badminton.

rink A marked section of ice used for sports such as ice hockey, curling and figure skating. A rink is also a strip of lawn used for lawn bowling.

rounders A team game of bat and ball in which players run the round of the bases. It is an older and more basic form of baseball.

runners A long set of blades, usually made of steel, on which a sled, toboggan or luge rides over ice.

scrimmage A play in American football that begins with two teams lined up opposing each other and the ball placed on the ground between them.

scrum or scrummage A grouping of rugby players. Players from one team bind together on one side and push against a similar grouping from the opposing team to win possession of the ball.

shuttlecock Weighted at one end, a shuttlecock is made of cork or plastic with a ring of feathers attached and is struck back and forth in the racket sport of badminton.

slalom In skiing or canoeing, a slalom event is conducted over a course that has a number of flags or artificial obstacles.

Team pursuit cyclists

sphairistike The first name given to the new sport of lawn tennis. It came from the Greek word "sphaira," which means ball.

stadium An enclosed sports ground, usually with banks of seats for spectators.

strike In basketball, a strike is an accurate pitch that the batter misses or chooses not to hit. In tenpin bowling, a strike is the knocking down of all the pins with one bowl.

striker A soccer player whose main task during the course of a game is to score goals.

stumped In cricket, a batsman is stumped when a player from the opposing team, usually the wicketkeeper, knocks the bails off the top of the stumps while the batsman is out of the crease.

stumps Three upright wooden pegs that form a set that is called a wicket in a game of cricket.

Super Bowl The grand final game to decide the annual National Football League championship of the United States. The word "bowl" is used to describe the large bowl-like stadium in which the game is played.

tee A cleared space of land from which the ball is struck at the beginning of each hole in a game of golf. A tee is also the name of the small plastic or wooden holder used to support the ball.

touchdown In American football, a team scores a touchdown by carrying the ball or receiving it over the opposing team's goal line.

try In rugby union and rugby league, players score a try by touching the ball down over their opponents' goal line.

vane A blade of feathers or plastic used to keep arrows and darts on a straight course.

velodrome An oval-shaped, banked track used for cycling events. A banked track has curved sides that slope steeply upwards.

wicketkeeper In the game of cricket, the wicketkeeper stands behind the batsman and the stumps and catches the balls that go past the batsman.

Golf caddie

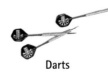

Darts

Canoeing safety equipment

63

Index

Picture Credits

(t=top, b=bottom, l=left, r=right, c=center, i=icon, F=front, C=cover, B=back, Bg=background)
Action Images, 37bc, **Action-Plus**, 25tr, 31tl (S. Bardens), 45tr (C. Barry), 15cr (D. Davies), 58bl (R. Francis), 29br (N. Haynes), 33cr (M. Hewitt), 14tl, 54bl (G. Kirk), 11tc (P. Tarry), 36bc. **Ad-Libitum**, 1, 4bl, 4tcr, 4tl, 4tr, 5tr, 8br, 10tl, 13cr, 14cl, 14bl, 17br, 26bl, 28bl, 28c, 28tl, 31bl, 31br, 33br, 33tc, 34c, 34tl, 34tr, 37br, 40bl, 46b, 48tl, 52tl, 58cl, 62bcl, 62bl, 62tl, 63bcr, 63br, 63tr (S. Bowey), 36bl, 36tr (S. Bowey/Benson Archery, Sydney). **AKG, London**, 38c (E. Lessing). **Art Resource**, 39tr (E. Lessing/The Louvre). **Australian Picture Library**, 44/45b, 44tl, 50tr (Agence Vandystadt/Allsport), 40tl (Agence Vandystadt/Allsport/ G. Planchenault), 49bl, 57tr (Agence Vandystadt/R. Martin), 38/39c (Agence Vandystadt/C.H. Petit), 59tl (Agence Vandystadt/P. Vielcanet), 19bl, 22tr, 48bl, 48tr (Allsport), 48/49c (Allsport/S. Bruty), 19bc, 59tr (Allsport/ D. Cannon), 10bl (Allsport/J. Gishigi), 52c (Allsport/B. Martin), 24tr, 42tr (Allsport/M. Powell), 51br (Allsport/P. Rondeau), 57cr (Allsport/A. Want), 47cr (Bettmann), 34cl (E.T. Archive), 41tr (ZEFA). **Oliver Berlin**, 33bc, 35cr, 35tl. **The Bridgeman Art Library**, 27tr (Marylebone Cricket Club),

56tcr (The New York Historical Society), 35tr. **The British Museum**, 19cl. **China Stock**, 9cr (C. Liu). **Colorsport**, 17tr, 18cl, 23tl. **D. Donne Bryant Stock**, 17bl (A. Zaloznik). **The Granger Collection**, 7cr, 15tc, 15tcr. **The Image Bank**, 7tr (Duomo), 24bl, 38bl (Duomo/D. Madison), 44bl (Duomo/W. Sallaz), 56tr. **Live Action**, 47tr, 52cl (V. Acikalin), 54c (SIPA-PRESS). **Mary Evans Picture Library**, 26br (R. Mayne), 12tl, 21tr, 30tl, 33tl, 38bc, 56tr. **Marylebone Cricket Club**, 27tc. **The Photo Library, Sydney**, 52tr (N. Green), 6bl, 23cr (Hulton Deutsch), 28bc (J. McCawley), 54tcl (TSW), 34/35c (TSW/D. Leah), 50tl (TSW/B. Torrez). **Robert Harding Picture Library**, 53tr (A. Evrard), 18tl (J. Thorne), 30br (A. Woolfitt & R. Tonkinson). **Sport The Library**, 26tcl (D. Braybrook), 44tcl (D. Callow), 50bl, 54tl, 57tl, 60bl (J. Crow), 61br (B. Frakes), 26tl (T. Nolan), 42tc (S. Perkins), 42bl (N. Schipper), 16tl (J. Wachter), 12bl, 13tr, 19tc, 43tc, 43tr, 60tl. **Sporting Pix**, 61tc (T. Feder), 37cr, 60tc, 61bl (Popperfoto), 8cl, 8tc, 19tl, 21tl, 42bc, 45tl, 60/61c (B. Thomas) 60br. **Dean Wilmot**, 50/51c.

Illustration Credits

Christer Eriksson, 14/15c, 24/25c, 54/55c. Chris Forsey, 18/23c.

Ray Grinaway, 4i, 5b, 6i, 8i, 10i, 12i, 13i, 14i, 15i, 16i, 18i, 24i, 26i, 28i, 29i, 30i, 31i, 32i, 34i, 36i, 48t, 49t, 50cl, 52b, 53tr, 53t, 62cl, endpapers. **Adam Hook/Bernard Thornton Artists, UK**, 8/9c, 8bl, 32/33c, 33tr. **Christa Hook/Bernard Thornton Artists, UK**, 6/7c, 6tl, 40/41c, 40tr, 41tl. **Janet Jones**, 42/43c, 56/57b. **Iain McKellar**, 26/27c, 30/31c, 63cr. **Steve Noon/Garden Studio**, 12/13c, 16/17c, 16bl. **Matthew Ottley**, 5i, 38i, 38tl, 38cl, 40i, 44i, 46i, 48i, 49i, 50i, 52i, 54i, 56i, 57i, 58i, 58/59c, 58tl, 62tcl. **John Richards**, 2, 19–22c, 36/37c, 46/47c, 47tr, 63tr. **Roger Stewart/Brihton Illustration**, 3, 10/11c, 11tr. **Rodger Towers/Brihton Illustration**, 28/29c.

Diagrams and Maps

Catherine Au-Yeung

Cover Credits

Ad-Libitum, FCcl, BCtr, Bg (S. Bowey). Ray Grinaway, FCtr, BCbl. John Richards, FCc.